AF251573

DAWN PEARL

POEMS BY

IRENE CHADWICK

CALLIGRAPHY BY JEAN McKEON
COVER BY ERIC CHADWICK

FOR LEE

~Your Gift~

I hold sacred
These Sunday afternoons

Placing your parchment iris ~
in a paper vase

Arranging my assumptions
into a poem

CHINA WALLS

CRUMBLING WALLS
OF LICHENED STONES
LAID ONE ON TOP OF ANOTHER
HUG THE RISING LINES
OF ROLLING HILLS.
I CAN SEE CHINAMEN
A CENTURY AGO
CARRYING EACH HEAVY STONE,
PLACING EACH ONE JUST SO
TO BALANCE THE SQUAT WALL
AGAINST THE RISE OF HILL.

COYOTE CALL
BEFORE THEY JAY WALK
THROUGH AMBER FOXTAILS
AND DISAPPEAR
OVER ANOTHER HILL.
DENSE OAKS STAND AS SQUAT
COMMANDERS IN THE SWEEP
OF DARKNESS CLOSING IN,
GUARDING THE SAGGING WALL.

EACH HILLTOP OAK BECOMES
A BLACK SILHOUETTE
AGAINST THE PALE
DROPPING OF SUNLIGHT
FROM THE BOWL
THAT ONCE WAS CHINA BLUE.

CRICKETS PLAY TAPS
ON GRAINS OF WILD OATS
THE BREEZE PICKS UP,
BEFORE RETREATING GENTLY
INTO TWILIGHT, CASTING
HUMAN IMAGES
FULL, SOLID, INDIVIDUAL
UPON THE WALL.

~Steaming Lump~

Blue crystals glinting off
Jack-Frosted storm windows
My small feet bare on cold linoleum
Her gentle chiding
What? No sox? No shoes?
As she puts a lump of brown sugar
Into my hot bowl of Cream of Wheat
I look up to her, then down.
Under my uncertain spoon the lump
Melting, begins to wear a smile.

Grandmother

Mysteriously shaped and fired
from precious kaolin
Blank white china
was sent to Grandmother
Before World War I
in sturdy wooden barrels
Each stamped Limoges Haviland

She painted violets
on each eggshell-thin teacup
Gold-scalloped
rims and edges
Fired each piece
in the crucible of
Earth Air Fire Water

After World War II
you come to me unafraid
Knowing I care
how fragile your strength
How delicate your alchemy —
A first-century Chinese puzzle

Your fine bones
I handle as jealously
guarded secret.
Your chemistry as mysterious
as that fine white clay
from France

Beeches: Point Reyes

I am a boy climbing
up the smooth skin
of a beechnut. My hands
grab the tattered
end of a rope. I swing
out over Bass Lake and
drop into its clear depths

I come up through the
sweet cold and drink in
the moving waters
with all my senses
alert. From this
perspective, water
is the only reality

I am a boy diving
from the cool skin of
white beeches into clear
lakes, a boy scampering
along the trail to its end
to see water falling
in sheets over the cliff

I am a boy who loves
the white washed sands
of pacific beaches
scrubbing my skin
clean, the warm
love skin of girls

Clothespin Dolls

Five stories below our clothesline
in Israel, doll-sized children
fashion dreams from scraps.
Abandoned plastic boxes
used to carry groceries home,
become box cars
pulled by a long rope
encircling the waist of a boy-engine.
One car carries a boy-traveller.
Another is piled high
with cracked-off chunks of sidewalk.
They load, pull, push,
weight cars to balance the ride,
screech over desert sand —
until some connection breaks.
Then, shouts and bits of wire from
the garbage bin get twisted into use.

In Iowa on the farm
  we often made our toys.
  Corncobs from the bushel basket
  of tinder drying near the iron stove,
  laid end-to-end on the cold linoleum,
  became roads to town, tractors
  in the cornfields, playhouses.
From the Singer sewing machine,
  cloth scraps fell
  to become fashions for clothespin dolls —
  boys in overalls, girls in dresses,
  mothers in aprons, papas in straw hats
  fashioned from real straw.
  String hair got combed
  with ragged fingernails. Blue crayola
  eyes, red lips — blurred dots, bits from
  the tinder bin twisted into connection.

Botany in the Bahamas

Flesh-swelling wind
    taps with drumsticks.
Like goatskin timpani
    everything tropical quivers:
Tamarind juice in
        golden goblets
Slow sweep of hibiscus into
        fan of Traveller's Palm
Cool blue jacaranda
        against long banana leaves
Royal poinciana with its
        scarlet umbrella of flames
Gossip wheezing from rattling
        seed pods of Woman's Tongue

—FREE DIRT—

Do not put my body in this unused park
of granite trees where vandals chip
REST IN PEACE to RUST IN PIECES,
dogs lift legs on Bible verses,
wildflowers bloom chill reminders
to speeders by who automatically
look away—before a shiver
travels down their spines
as they read FREE DIRT,
clear sign of where
they've come from, where
they're speeding to

Aubade —

When I return I practice portion control.
On granola sprinkle fresh nutmeg,
forego the honey. During my absence
the lilac has come into bloom,
black crow become more intelligent.
The river gentling by, as always,
cradles tadpoles in her pockets.
Drake and hen bathe.

In the lovely silences of a new day
I remember my body—how it swayed
to the music of one hundred women,
how eagle soared to native lore,
how mouse found the jacket I left behind
and brought it to me in the nick of time.

In the window above the kitchen sink
bear stares me in the face —
she, the very last leaf to fall
from the top of the plane tree.
Buffalo stride by
studying tiny forget-me-nots.
Each bud on each twig swells each
neuron in woman head.
It is the time of leafing out.

Why question what flowers
I might blossom into, what new buds.
Iris touches the smooth cock of morning.
It is enough to work, to love,
be borne up on woman spirit.
Distance cannot divide, separate,
diminish our power. The fish, the fowl,
air, water and flowers leap up — sing.
Fire is among us.

Double Exposure

My only daughter is walking
   uphill on cobblestones
Through the Jaffa Gate
   into the old walled city

Busy traffic is lightened
   by an occasional moonbeam
Spiraling through the din
   of dusky intentions
Evening—piled high with spare tires
   sewer lids
Sunlight splashing
   doubly-exposed curves

When will The Holy City
   loosen its rocks?
The stone faces of Jerusalem
   crack open?
Wondering centuries clasp to their bosom
   slender moonbeams?

Bride's Bouquet

Wearing her mother's
gown and her father's
blessing, she lifts
lace orchids that
spring from lichen
cradled in the
Rock of Ages.
Leaves flutter.
Memories smile.

Magic dwells
within the pearls
she flings
over her head
into the hands
of tomorrow.

Mali Baby

In Timbucktu below the Sahara
a goat wanders about
in a small mud hut
bumping into something—
fingers, flies or feces.
Black flies swarm
over a baby's face
eating the dirty mucous
oozing out of swollen eyes
and nose—even though
his mother keeps him moving.
When the baby dies
his voice will not be missed.

Climbing a rock mountain
above the Red Sea,
suddenly I see again
those helpless hands.
I rise up slowly.
At the barren top
new views emerge—Arabia,
Jordan, Egypt's Sinai,
its land bridge a swollen face
between the ponderous hands
of Asia and Africa.
In my room that night
I cannot rest.
My body aches to cradle his.

Darkness

Out of darkness comes everything I need
Flowers – the rare ghost-white
phantom orchid,
skull cap of the wild onion,
the edible death camas
with Diogenes' lantern.
I look into their dark eyes
and see petals in my reflection.

Rage possesses danger
runs like wildfire through treetops
undoing the pretences of light.
No one suspects who is the arsonist.

Under the ocean is abundance —
one tongue of coral that plunges
straight down into the deepest valley,
sea cucumbers vacuuming up the sand.
Laughter emerges from dark lungs.
Ecstacy from entombed wombs
Each little death is a dream turned round.

ancestors

in her eyes become
birds and fishes
sticks and stones
bodies and bones
whirling around
her world with

myth and sky
sea and sand,
hair of life
rising from
dark crevice,
solid rock –
light biding its time

LOCKED WARD

THE IRREVERSIBLY
SHRIVELED-UP OLD
HUNCHED ON SCUFFED
WOODEN BENCHES,
PASSING THE LAST
DAYS OF THEIR LIVES
IN THE PRISONS
OF THEIR MINDS;
CONFINED TO DISCARDED
PEWS IN A DAY ROOM,
SHUFFLING ALONG HALLWAYS
SMELLING OF DRIED-UP
FECES AND URINE.
THE OLD,
TIED TO A BED
OR A CHAIR,
HAIR WILDLY UNKEMPT
CLOTHES ASKEW
EYES SAD, WEARY,
PLEADING, HELP ME
LEAVE THIS HELL.

~ On The Evening Mother Dies ~

Only now — this once —
this little stream is slowed into
one thin sinew of a lake
its glassy eye reflecting
every black tangle of twig at sunset

Lengthening shadows of evening
steal skylight from the water
smooth as glass, still as death
Not even one sensuous ripple disturbs
the solemnity of this moment

～ FLYING ～

I LOVE TO FLY ANY TIME ANYWHERE
ANY PLACE WITH ANYONE IN ANY KIND
OF MACHINE — EVEN ON MY OWN ALL
ALONE. FLYING DOWN A SNOWY MOUNTAIN
ON LONG BOARD FEET I GO SO FAST IT

FEELS LIKE I'VE GOT WINGS. THE WIND
WHOOSHES THROUGH MY HAIR. JOY LIFTS
MY PARKA. I RECALL CATCHING FLY BALLS
A FOOTBALL ARCHING UP LIKE WATER FROM
A FIRE HOSE.   I SEE A PAIR OF DOVE

COAX TWO FLEDGLINGS OUT OF THE NEST
ONTO THE WIDE LIMB'S CRACKED BARK.
WHEN THEY FLY AWAY I FEEL A SUDDEN
SADNESS DEEP INSIDE. MY PAPER PRAYERS
WILL HOLD UP A SON FLYING OVER THE

OCEAN TONIGHT. I STOP BREATHING SEEING
ANOTHER SON ON HIS SOLO FLIGHT,
WOBBLY WINGS NEARLY SOMERSAULTING INTO
THE RUNWAY. I SEE MY ONLY DAUGHTER DEEP
SEA DIVING INTO MONTEREY BAY, SHARKS

FLYING FROM UNDERWATER MOUNTAIN PEAKS
TOWARD HER. I SEE TWO BROTHERS LIVING
THEIR LIVES IN FLYING MACHINES.
STRANGE KINDS OF WINGS SURROUND THEIR
SOFT BODIES: HELICOPTER BLADES

BLURRED AS THE HUMMINGBIRD'S. A STUNT
PLANE'S RED WINGS TUMBLING TOWARD EARTH.
GLIDER WINGS FLOATING THROUGH NIMBUS
CLOUDS. SILVER WINGS AS SHINY IN THE
SUN AS ICARUS' WAX WINGS. STANDING IN

THE BASKET OF A HOT AIR BALLOON IN
FRANCE I SEE ITS SHADOW BECOME A
FOOTBALL IN THE CANAL BELOW AND LOVE
THE EXHILARATION OF BURSTING FORTH FROM
THIS OLD EARTH, CASTING MY ENERGY ABROAD.

~Path of the Padres~

Tied thumb-to-thumb Yokut Indians
tramped a Trail of Tears up
Arroyo de Los Banos Del Padre Arroyo
over the Diablo Range —
Captured to become neophytes
at San Juan Bautista Mission,
until malaria wiped them out.

Hands linked we snake up
trickling Los Banos Creek
Straining up this narrow canyon
destined to be dammed, unless another
endangered species can be found —
Elderberry's bark boring beetle
having failed to qualify

From poison oak a deer bolts straight
up the opposite hill over Nutgrass —
Yokut Indian name for themselves.
Cliff swallows dive bomb
from mud nests. Star thistles
bloom plush purple, cherry red

Yellow trumpets announce California's
tobacco bush to the falcon's gyre.
From ancient white sycamore
killdeer wing up crying Danger—
which species next?

Dawn
a pink pearl
large and luminous
silent and wet
before the rain of

Day
a rough oyster shell
holding mottled flesh
wet and grey, quivering
the grit of sand grains
running through its succulence
quick dissolving
into the dust of

Night
large and black, a coal
its embers flickering

— Walking Up Wildcat Canyon —

Sunlight darts through viscosities to reveal
pollen shifting over the murky surfaces,
slow paddle of turtle legs underwater.
Son's eyes see what parents pass by —

Four large turtles in sleepy slouch
on dead logs held above water,
webbed with refuse and the
steady dissonance of accumulations.

Poignant melodies weave through our bifocal
lenses, shells protecting visceral lumps.
Past Red-eared slider turtles we climb
through wooded tunnel.

Barreling along next to the invisible
way of the wildcat, long paddling
paws, we are becoming
visceral lumps upon encrusted logs.

Spirits

Twenty two balloons
in the morning sky
Twenty two balloons
go floating by
Twenty two balloons
in the pale blue breeze
Wakened from slumber
with a hot air sneeze
Lifting our spirits
beyond our sight
Lifting our bodies
from the dark of night

Burnished Leaves

You lift my chemise,
uncover concave bowl of belly.
Moons rise from lunarscape of craters.
Serpentine riffs ride wide the strath,
flow through tidal flats tracing concave
sockets, close-swat interiors.

We eat a bowl of cherries,
drink wine from goblets.
The glow of late-day stars
scatter seed from pole to pole.
Your sun swizzles around my moons.
Daylight yawns into moonlight. Outside,
a woodpecker fondles last year's walnut.

Into the black pit all lovers go we descend,
tonguing the language of obscurities.
Rip-rhythms, gentle cadences, crescendo
to the crush of some faraway jazz,
we become piercing needles of light.
Stitched velvet to silk, fur to burlap
we unravel so slowly. Fall back
from the pit through panes of glass.
Outside, new tufts, little fountains of
burnished leaves sprouting Serpent's Tongues.

— FROM SEA TO SHINING SEE —

YOUR MOTHER DIES.
WIFE LEAVES YOU FOR ANOTHER.
BROKE, YOU RACE FROM ATLANTIC
TO PACIFIC ON A MOTORCYCLE.
TURNING TO GOD
YOU BEGIN TO WRITE AND SKETCH,
GET THE CATHOLIC CHURCH TO ANNUL
THE LONG MARRIAGE,
DECIDE TO BECOME A JESUIT.

SONS COME OF AGE. YOUR FATHER DIES.
ENOUGH IS ENOUGH.
MARY COMES TO MOTHER YOU,
I CAN UNDERSTAND.
WHEN WE COME TO VISIT
WE SEE YOUR SNAPSHOT,
FRAMED IN THE BEDROOM MIRROR,
BLACK FROM HEAD TO TOE
THRUST FORWARD ON YOUR CYCLE

ABOVE YOUR BED, A STREET SIGN —
SURVEY PARTY. COVERING YOUR WALLS —
LACED-UP VIRGINS, ANGELIC WHORES.
YOUR SAINTS AND SINNERS TROUBLE ME.
IN THE NIGHT I WRITE.
MY MOTHER DIED THAT SAME YEAR,
FATHER SOON AFTER.
SOMEONE I NEEDED LEFT AND WROTE
NEVER AGAIN CONTACT ME.

MY FRIEND, I HAVE LEARNED THAT
LIFE CANNOT BE ANNULLED.
EVEN DEATH WILL NOT STOP ITS THROBBING.
IN SOME WAYS OUR POEMS ARE PRAYERS
WE PLACE UPON THE ALTAR OF LIFE —
WAFER-THIN, BLOOD-RED LOGOS
POSITIONED LIKE STOLEN SIGNS
SURVEYING SILENT SINS.

A LITTLE DRUNK AT THE COUNTRY CLUB

WHEN I FALL ON MY ASS
AT THE EDGE OF THE FLOOR
AND TWO OF THE DOCTORS HEAVE HO!
HEAVE HO! AND I'M BACK IN THE
WHIRL IN THE PSYCHIATRIST'S ARMS
SELF CONSCIOUS AS HELL BUT WHAT-THE-HELL
ME ON THE MAKE, HIM NOT ON THE TAKE

AFTER TWENTY YEARS OF SPOUSAL SUPPORT
YOU CALL US GIRLS? HOLY SHIT! HOLY SHIT!
WE'RE WOMEN UPHOLDING YOU GREAT WHITE FATHERS
WOMEN OF FORTUNE, WOMEN ILL-FRAMED, WE
PLAY YOUR GAME   WE PLAY YOUR GAME
YOUR LOVERS AND WIVES, MOTHERS AND NURSES

WE PLAY YOUR GAME, UNTIL WE FALL FLAT
AT THE ANNUAL CHRISTMAS DANCE OF CHANCE
THESE MILES GOING HOME, GOING HOME IN THE DARK
THERE'S SHEETS OF TEARS AS I THINK ALL THE TIME
IT'S USELESS SELF-PITY, USELESS AND DUMB
MY BLACK AND BLUE, BUT...

— Woolgathering —

With the pink flush of dawn
dreams of you leave
their rosy cheeks upon the pillow.
We rise all of us together,
to see our lives woven
into a giant tapestry
hanging on a sunny wall
in the Smithsonian —

Sheep's wool carded
with curved combs
disentangled, cleansed
its scent the wool wax
of our animal past
gyrating fiercely...
Fluff emerging into fiber
Each woof breath of our lives
twisting into yarns —
dream mind of a common consciousness.

Hetch Hetchy Valley: Yosemite

In the dark grotto even the rocks weep
as we lie under their chill beauty.
The steady drip of ferns
cuts rock in half.
Drinking wine we let memory
flood feeling. Far below lies
O'Shaughnessy's mammoth dam
holding up ten miles of
flooded Tuolumne
for San Francisco's Irish thirst.
Half your melodies lie buried,
Hetch Hetchy. Granite cathedrals,
half domes hidden
this Grand Canyon is gone.

We emerge to the glare of quartz
in mountains too steep to climb,
their polished mirrors startle

Wind bursting open clouds
Trout pools
lit by Indian paintbrush
The monolithic music of a single grotto
commemorating droughts and human thirsts
Black lichen in long signatures
left as letters from another world

Is only one grotto left?
One icicle
pristinely placed
between boulders
and crashing falls?
One diamond
left glittering
between fire and ice?

—Pa and Me—

Polymorphous forces—Pa and Me.
Not floating states from vapor to air
slowly congealing into drops of rain
crystallizing into the skating pond
on Washington Park Lake. My four-foot-
long wool stocking cap streaming behind in
hopes 13-year-old Herman Guichelaar will tug.

No, I'm not fluid.
Ice crashes into the lake
Vapor sweats off my skinny arms—
sticks pulling at oars—
boiling up waves. I see a
lurking whirlpool pulling me under
into its murky Stygian abyss.
Welter of pawky Pa and Me—maladroit child.

I struggle to overcome the
tide of tears welling up,
bitten back, concealed, congealing ashore
into a stone-face cheer.   The ground
under Pa's wheelchair grows rough,
tugs at the wheels. Impeded he slows,
grinds to a halt. Gently I push, hear
blades hiss on ice, ground-out steel from
his clenched teeth: I'll do it myself.

~Golubka's 1993 USA Tour~

2 a.m. and now some large Russian
upstairs opens his bedroom door
and clomp clomps down the hall
interrupting dreams of steamy booths
covered and crowded, foreigners,
mingling gypsies, each booth a people.
These Russians want detente, no less.
That's why they came to America.
They want us, them, the Germans
to turn sexual conquest, lust for
land, suspicion, into hands extended
across oceans. Approach each other
with only our ears cocked. They want
everything, everyone to wake up

— GOLUBKA IS RUSSIAN FOR PEACE, DOVE, CARRIER PIGEON. —

～TENDER FLOCK～

WALKING UNDERWATER I LET
MY BROTHERS DIRECT ME
INTO A LARGE ROOM CLOAKED IN
NIGHT. UNDERWATER I MUST CUT
SO MANY BEAUTIFUL FLOWERS
ALL FRAGILE. THE LONG SLENDER
STEMS FILLED WITH WATER AND
LIGHT ARE SOFT AND POROUS.

IN THE DARK I DO THIS.
CUT THEM DEEP TAKING CARE
NOT TO BRUISE THEIR TENDER
STEMS. SMALL BLUE KNOTS
ORANGE POPPIES CONVOLUTED
PINK BUNCHES OF SWEET WILLIAM.
PURPLE MYSTERIES, BUTTERFLIES
RELEASED A TENDERLY SHORT
TIME INTO THE BREEZE.

IN THE DARK ROOM IS A WIZENED
OLD MAN, HIS THINNING WHITE
BEARD SPLENDID SILK FLOWING
CLEAR TO THE FLOOR. I MUST HELP
HIM FIND HIS WAY. WHEN I LEAVE
THE ROOM THE PRICE I MUST PAY
TO TAKE THE CUT FLOWERS HOME IS
TOO GREAT SO I LEAVE THEM THERE.

TO SEE THE EARLY MORNING
LIGHT IN A NEW FIELD BEYOND
THE ROAD, EYES MUST SWIM
THROUGH BLOSSOMS, NOT A
BLAZING TREE ON FIRE,
BUT THE SMALLEST NEW PLUM
TREE, EACH TINY BUD OPENING
A FLOCK OF TENDER TWIGS
FLOATING ABOVE A GREEN VALLEY.
ONE BUD FROM THE TENDER FLOCK
TURNS INTO A LAMB AND TAKES
THE BENT WIZARD FROM TWIG TO LOG.

~ Almond Blossom Snow ~

Every February white sentries appear
to guard the rag tag regiments
on the scraggly hills and
flood plain across the creek.
Suddenly they appear
in a quite charming fashion
bursting into bloom overnight.
From her distant perch on this side
she counts them — one, two, three,
four, then more arrivals stark-white,
singular, pristine behind and among
the wildness of bare-twisted branches

Every year she waits for them to appear.
They share an unspoken code of honor —
they guard their side, she guards her's.
When their tour of duty is done
off come their white uniforms,
on go their drab khakis,
but her tour of duty never ends.
She never stops looking at the
signature of legend on almond bark

That teenage German princess
given in marriage to Portugal's
Prince Philip, gazing from castle
turret each winter, longing for snow
and her Northern home. Each January
her prince would see her pining,
waiting at the window. So he
commanded the whole countryside
planted in almond orchards —
and then he waited

Each January he would drive her
in the royal coach through the
falling almond blossom snow
in hopes of her ardour returning,
drifting south like blown snow
into his Principality of Portugal.
The legend does not tell
what really happened to them

Meadow Symphony

Beyond a high trail
soft grass covers the remains
of the Eldorado Hotel.
No one is here or anywhere near
when I lie down to rest.
Even though I grow so still
that the coming of slow
breathing feels intrusive,
my presence disturbs everything.

After long enough
the natural order
of living things
resumes its ways.
The strangeness of stillness
passes. Around my body
the landscape opens up.
Sounds of meadow life seep

I am beginning
to pick out each voice
of the meadow symphony
when sudden thunder

opens the lightning sky.
If I stand up
in this high bare place
my body will become
a lightning rod.

Waiting flat and still
under the falling cloud
I am grounded.
I know where I am.
The rain will pass.

Forthcoming from the
Ietje Kooi Press is
MOTHER: SON OF SAM by
the Four Kooi Sisters